Social Media Domination: How you can strive and survive on Platforms likeFacebook, Twitter, Instagram and YouTube

By: Ted Dawson

©Copyright 2017 WE CANT BE BEAT LLC.

Copyright 2017 by Ted Dawson.

Published by WE CANT BE BEAT LLC

Krob817@yahoo.com

Table of Contents

Social Media Domination 1
   How you can Strive and Survive on Platforms like. 1
   Facebook, Twitter, Instagram and YouTube 1

Introduction 8

Chapter 1 - Manage a social media campaign 15

Chapter -2 – Content Sharing and Effectiveness 27

Chapter 3 – Understanding Social Media 40

Understanding Twitter 40

Understanding Facebook 48

Monetize your business using Linkedin, Tumbler, Pinterest, Google + ... 55
   Google + ... 56
   LinkedIn 61
   Tumblr 67
   Pinterest 69

Chapter 4 - 6 Google Marketing Tools You Should Be Using 72

Chapter 5 - Video/ YouTube Marketing 86

Chapter 6 - Integrate social media with your website 93
   Monetize through Instagram 96

Chapter 7 - Wrapping up social media with newsletters and PR...107

Chapter 8 - Mobile Marketing 114

   Harvesting leads & sales from mobile 118

   The Wonders of WhatsApp 121

Chapter 9 - Social media metrics 124

Conclusion 135

This document is geared towards providing exact and reliable information in regards to the topic and issues covered. The publication is sold on the idea that the publisher is not required to render an accounting, officially permitted, or otherwise, qualified services. If advice is necessary, legal or professional, a practiced individual in the profession should be ordered.

From a Declaration of Principles which was accepted and approved equally by a Committee of the American Bar Association and a Committee of Publishers and Associations.

In no way is it legal to reproduce, duplicate, or transmit any part of this document by either electronic means or in printed format. Recording of this publication is strictly prohibited and any storage of this document is not allowed unless with written permission from the publisher. All rights reserved.

The information provided herein is stated to be truthful and consistent, in that any liability, in terms of inattention or otherwise, by any usage or abuse of any policies, processes, or directions contained within is the solitary and utter responsibility of the recipient reader. Under no circumstances will any legal responsibility or blame be held against the publisher for any reparation, damages, or monetary loss due to the information herein, either directly or indirectly.

Respective authors own all copyrights not held by the publisher.

The information herein is offered for informational purposes solely and is universal as so. The presentation of the information is without a contract or any type of guarantee assurance.

The trademarks that are used are without any consent, and the publication of the trademark is without permission or backing by the trademark owner. All trademarks and brands within this book are for clarifying purposes only and are owned by the owners themselves, not affiliated with this document.

Introduction

1. In 2009 Christen Dominique rushed home to cook her husband's favorite meal so that they could celebrate their first month of togetherness in fine style. With aromatic candles and fresh flowers decorating the living room, she was ready to try out the new weight loss recipe of pumpkin pie. As she was preparing the dish she realized that she forgot the measure of ingredients. Her first thought was to call up her mom. Then she remembered that her mom was away cruising with friends. Her next solace was YouTube. She flipped her phone and reached to the video sharing site for pumpkin pie recipe. Within seconds she could watch the video and dish out a lip smacking recipe. That is when the idea struck her to start a channel on YouTube for her business.

Christen who is 30 years old, was a freelance makeup artist who was paid a meager $30 per hour. Though she could make ends meet Christen wasn't happy with her modest lifestyle. When one of her clients asked her to show how to apply lipstick to get fuller lips, Christen felt she should upload the video on YouTube. That was the beginning of much more make-up tutorials and today Christen has more than 6 million followers. She promotes her videos through her Facebook, Twitter and Instagram accounts. Several companies that sell beauty products approach her to promote their products. Her net worth is more than a million dollar and Christen is today rich and famous. This is a true story of how a commonor rose to become famous, thanks to social media.

2. When Joanne was given the pink slip she didn't know what to do. She was a packaging manager at an electronic store.

The chain of store closed down leaving many like Joanne jobless. Her friend advised her to use her contacts she developed in her job for sourcing of electronic goods and Joanne made a website to sell her products online. She started promoting the products on her Facebook page as well as Twitter. She sent newsletters regularly through email marketing and also made announcements through Facebook forums. She also joined many community pages where she could showcase her products. She updated the product page, offered freebies, and discounts, soon people started trooping to her E-commerce site.

She even joined Instagram (free) and promoted her goods. She made thousands of 'friends' on Facebook and 'followed' many on Twitter and Instagram. With one update she could reach out to thousands of people. She offered discounts during the holiday seasons and the rush was visible on her site. Today, Joanne is a busy woman with more than 2000 'hits' per day.

The world welcomed the 21st century with internet and in a decade social media became a craze. Orkut was the first social media site started in 2004 where you could interact with your friends both near and far. It was eventually bought by Google and soon died a quiet death. Facebook was started in 2006; the next year Twitter followed and the social world exploded. Facebook, Twitter, Instagram, Snapchat, Tumblr, Pinterest, Google +, LinkedIn are some of the popular social media sites today. Anyone and everyone is on social media and the power it holds is phenomenal. Twitter's 140 characters have the power to bring down a government. American President Donald Trump used Twitter to reach out to the public during elections and still does so to air his views. The major advantage of social media is the instant speed at which your posts goes viral. The entire world becomes aware of what you were or are doing within a matter of minutes.

The beauty of social media is, it is free and anybody can join. All you need is your smartphone or PC to 'sign in' and create a profile. There are more than 1 billion users on Facebook. It is as good as a virtual world of its own. Though it started out as a friendly photo sharing site it is now catering to businesses as well. There was a time when businesses made websites and promoted them through other mediums like television and print. The cost for promoting their products was high. Thanks to social media the cost is negligible now and you can even promote your product for free. The ROI (return on investment) is phenomenal and businesses find it easy to use.

This ebook is a sincere attempt to help you understand the absolute power of social media domination and how you can harness it to develop your business. The secret tips mentioned here will help you to strive and thrive in this highly competitive world where businesses are struggling hard to get themselves seen and heard. This book will help you to start a blog and demonstrate to you on how you can automatically make it known on your social media handles about the latest update. Your blog will automatically update your social media handles.

It is important to understand the opportunities, limitations, and differences to be able to develop a strategy on how you are going to use these mediums to achieve your objectives and set reasonable expectations. Social media encompasses texting, video sharing, photo sharing, music sharing, podcasts, blogs, forums and communities that are available online.

This book will discuss in details about how you can harness the power of all these above-mentioned mediums to promote your business (small or large) and attain success with your venture. So, go on, read this book and get started on your success journey!

Chapter 1 - Manage a social media campaign

Jack wanted to start an online store for shoes. His family had been into leather shoe business for three generations. Their loyal customers came back to buy more of their stuff and often praised the staff for the quality of their shoes. Jack had heard that social media would be perfect for advertising. The question was pretty simple yet tough to answer. Social media was certainly the place to go but which platform should he choose? Google organic search looked promising. Facebook was an attractive option. Some of his friends suggested Twitter, but he had no clue how to make use of it. Of course, there was Instagram, Pinterest, Snapchat, Viber, Reddit and much more other social media channels to choose from. Jack realized that social media marketing was not as easy as it seemed from the outside.

Does social media marketing work?

Sometimes you get a feeling that social media is a lot of hot air. Nothing wrong if you feel that way. Who can believe that you can advertise your products and services free of cost? Who can believe that you can compete with the big bad boys who have loads of money to throw on social media campaigns? Actually, it's the other way around. Social media is a big equalizer. Now a small boy can stand up to a big bully. Large corporations, who used to steamroll their opinion through big budget advertisements on television and massive hoarding on every street corner, are now finding it difficult to compete with small players. Marketing is no longer about push but pull. You can't simply push your product to gullible folks who doesn't know any better than to believe in TV advertisements. Maybe around twenty years back you could be fooled when the only opinions were those of your neighbor or office colleague. Now the internet is full of reviews, feedback, ratings and experiences. Big corporates have lost their power. It takes but a few words to create or destroy a brand. User experience is the boss and no one can push the customer around. This is the power of social media.

Comprehensive social media strategy

Selling shoes online may not look like a brilliant idea in the first place. People need to see if the shoes fit is proper, right? Online shoe purchases can be dicey, right? Wrong. Social media marketing is all about forgetting the conventional and embracing the modern. Forget the past. Don't cling to the shoe sizes. Change the way you think. These were the lessons which John had to learn before stepping foot on his online shoe journey. Take the case of Zappos, a shoe seller online. They started on a shoestring budget of $2 million in 2000. Nine years down the (on) line, Zappos was bought by Amazon for a fat $940 million in a stock and cash deal. Now, who says that shoes can't be sold online? For that matter, anything and everything can be sold profitably on the internet and social media is a major part of it all.

You get the sense of it but how do you convert your idea into practice? Jack, to begin with, was a shoe manufacturer – not an online marketer. He did not want to spend all his savings on some fancy idea. The question which bothered him was simple – how do I manage my social media engagements? You would be surprised to know that even a rookie can master social media if he or she has the will to do it. The trick is to understand all aspects of this wonderful platform and implement whatever is necessary. But most of all, you must avoid stepping into the shoes which are irrelevant to your niche. For example, LinkedIn is a great social media site, but it's no good for selling shoes. What is LinkedIn good for, you may ask? You will learn about various social media platforms in detail later in this book. Suffice to say that each social media platform has its advantages and disadvantages.

Choosing the right combination of social media platforms

To begin with, Jack was confronted with a plethora of alternatives. He had to first set up an e-commerce site from where he could sell shoes. There are many kinds of e-commerce tools available in the market, which posed a new type of problem. What to choose and what to reject? He soon realized that ease of use must be his primary concern. Customers should be able to browse shoes and must be able to pay online without much effort. Like charity, social media begins at home. How user-friendly is your website? Can buyers place an order without struggling with the payment gateway? How can customers be sure that your site is secure? Even the best shoe with the lowest price will not be bought unless the customer is sure that his bank details are secure while transacting business with you.

Having designed a great e-commerce site, the next step for jack was to get people to visit the site. This is where social media stepped in. You got to put on the right shoes to go on an adventure. You also have to take the right steps. The process of selection depends on the product or service that you are selling. In other words, you must begin with your product. Jack realized that his customers were the types who like to be on Facebook. Engaging them on their favorite social media platform was a no brainer. But was this enough to get customers queuing up at his online store? Obviously not. Someone suggested to him that a blog would be a nice addition to his website. To start a blog is easy as long as you have good content to attract eyeballs. Who would create the content, he thought. Jack knew that he himself was not a writer. When he discussed the idea with his staff, he was surprised to learn that many employees volunteered to post on the blog. This not only built up the team spirit but also resulted in blog posts which were unique and relevant. When you start on your online journey, like Jack, you will often find surprises like this. Social media campaigns turn out to be magical and like a fairy tale – as long as you take the first baby steps with care.

Forge relationships on social media

Jack realized that social media engagements are not a one-day affair. You need commitment and patience- something like having a serious love affair. You have to build relationships over a period of time. There are no one-night-stands out here. There is a mistaken belief that once you have a Facebook account you can lie down and relax. Unfortunately, things don't happen that way. Social media campaigns have to be sustained over a long period of time. The term used is 'engagement.' How do you keep your customers interested? This is the first question which should pop up in your mind. You have to fall back to traditional marketing techniques. Keeping your customers happy is an art which works even today. Remember the 4 P's – Price, Product, Promotion, and Place. You might have firsthand experience of participating in online shopping. What do you remember about it? Pricing always wins especially when you are dealing with a product like shoes. Your product, of course, must speak for itself. The best part about social media is the word-of-mouth marketing. Word spreads like wildfire when you offer something attractive. This is also called viral marketing – when your customers become your best salespeople.

Coming back to the relationship issue, it takes time and considerable effort to make your presence felt in social media. You have to be at it constantly. Once your presence is acknowledged, your audience will experience a cascading effect. Friends of friends of friends will recommend your product and you will start attracting customers out of the blue. Don't expect this to happen within a day or week or even a month. Maturation takes much longer and a year seems like a good target.

Relationships are built brick by brick. It takes time to build a reputation online but a single bad review can bring down your house in an instant. You should always have a strategy to counter negative review. Offering immediate refund without asking questions can lead to redemption. Beware of your competitors trying to malign you by planting bad reviews. Social media marketing can be vicious and often is. Don't think it's a lovey-dovey place where love flows uninterrupted. On the other hand, you don't have to do anything new. You don't have to discover new strategies. Simply look at your successful competitor and create a template. It's a very simple and effective strategy. Social media marketing can turn out to be simple if you are smart.

You must also engage your audience seamlessly over many social media platforms. If you want to announce a discount, you should consider looking at Twitter. At the same time, you may like to engage your customers on Facebook, though you may not get an instant response. Events like clearance and flash sales are occasions to drum up sales. Here, time is of the essence. In such situations, an email newsletter may not work as well as Twitter. Long term social media engagements must be punctuated by small tactical bursts of tweets. This will allow you to maintain the excitement and freshness of your marketing campaign. Let your customers anticipate the next tweet while you feed them with regular news through other platforms.

Understanding social media

Jack soon came to know that using social media like Facebook for fun and using it for business are two different things. You should not be afraid of making mistakes, but having said that, your marketing campaign can flounder for months if you don't know how the ecosystem works. You should not assume that you know all about Facebook, just because you are using it. Of course, you will start off well if your awareness level is good. To excel in social media marketing you must go into the details of each platform. Twitter is a totally different ball game compared to Instagram. Both are effective platforms for marketing but have a different approach.

Therefore, you should not be afraid to get your feet dirty in the social pond. In fact, the more you learn, the more you will be able to come up with winning strategies. Consider this book as a great start and then dive deep into the subject. Don't think that social media is easy. It's is easy but only when you have in-depth knowledge.

Case of blind men and the elephant

One of the issues which jack had to grapple with was to know whether his online strategy was working or not. Accounting inside a physical shop was easy. He knew the number of people who visited his shop and those who went on to buy. This gave him a good idea about the effectiveness of his sales staff. Finding conversion rates for his online store was essential to him. Jack remembered a story which his father was fond of repeating.

Once upon a time, in a remote village, five blind men were asked to touch an elephant and suggested what it looked like. The first blind man touched the tail and said that it definitely looked like a rope. The blind man who touched the body claimed that an elephant looked like a wall. Every one of the blind men evaluated the elephant in a different manner. The lesson from this story is that you should not base your opinions on a single factor but look at any situation as a whole. Numbers by themselves may not reveal the whole story. Social media metrics is a subject to which one whole chapter has been devoted. Suffice to say that you have to take a comprehensive view when looking at the effectiveness of your campaign.

Chapter -2 – Content Sharing and Effectiveness

What is your story?

Finally, it all boils down to your story and how compelling it looks. What compelling story can you create from a shoe business? A shoe is a shoe, after all. Not really. Look for inspiration from Zappos. They are a shoe company but have great content. More than that, they have a story to tell.

Content strategy looks scary and technical, but it turns out that it is all the stuff your every day is made of. If you are telling a story of your customer, it means content strategy. Content means customer experience. Maybe you can embellish your story a little – to make it more interesting, but in the end, it's simple. You can throw a bit of search engine optimization, keywords, branding and you have a great content strategy.

You have heard this before - social media is about people and engagement. Unfortunately, we are so busy pushing our product that we forget the basics. Your customer will only respond when he or she gets that oooh feeling. This can only happen when you give them words with meaning, which means content.

What are the essential elements of great content? Firstly content itself and the people who create the content. You need passionate people. There is no substitute. Fortunately, in social media marketing, your customer is likely to create this content if she feels fired enough.

Looking closer into content, observe the substance. The tone and tenor make a difference. You need style. These components make up the substance. And then you have a structure which means coherence.

What did this mean to Jack? His approach was rather simple. Even in traditional sales, it has always been about the customers and who were these customers - simple folk looking for a pair of comfortable shoes. Perhaps a majority of them had low literacy levels. The content had to match the level of the audience. Jack made sure that there was nothing fancy about the content.

Asking the right questions

Jack was a shrewd salesman and knew the right questions to ask. Social media marketing is no different than normal marketing. The customers are the same whether online or otherwise. The five important questions according to John were

Who are the customers?

What are they looking for?

Why are they at the store?

When to close sales?

Where is the customer coming from?

Something new for an online store

There were two major differences between his brick and mortar store and the online avatar. His online store could be viewed on a PC and/or mobile. For his mobile version of the online store, he planned a compact look and feel. Headlines, highlights and the link to his website. That's all for his mobile content. For his website, he had a more elaborate plan.

The second important aspect which jack noticed was the need for keywords. Google search forms an important part of online marketing and the key to good search ranking are keywords. Content can be super effective but if you don't appear on the first page of search results, you are doomed. Jack also realized that finding the most effective keywords is not rocket science – anyone with a little bit of common sense can come up with a great list of keywords.

User content is the best content

Have you noticed that social media like Facebook and Twitter have no original content? Everything is user generated and consumed by the user. It's these stories which you have to flush out of your customers. Maybe, it is a story of how someone spent his holidays fishing in Alaska. Or a customer spending time on a safari in South Africa. These are the real stories which interest us. How is this going to help in selling shoes? Social media is not about business. You have to understand this concept well. People gather around a campfire to listen to stories. This has been happening since the days when we were hunter-gatherers. No one talks about business around a campfire. Social media is today's campfire. People visit Facebook when the want to hear stories of people. If you are planning to sell your product through social media, you better understand that you have to tell interesting stories which engage your audience which is there primarily to have fun. You have to slip in your message literally.

One of the important aspects which must be kept in mind is the control over your content. You may lose your way if you are too frivolous. This can lead to failure of your social media marketing campaign. You must therefore constantly channelize your content keeping the end goal in sight. Your message, even though subtle, must remain your focus. A great way to do this is to have an event calendar.

You must seed a story which is likely to be picked up by the audience. You can ask for people to post inspiring stories and announce a gift for the best inspirational story. You will find many inspiring stories which motivate and engage others. By seeding the idea or concept, you always remain in control of your content.

More importantly, people want to share their own stories on social media. This is where you have to harness the power of the general audience. You have a range of formats to deliver content. A single picture is worth a thousand words. You have a video which is much more powerful than an image. You must experiment with various formats till you come up with a winning formula. Embracing social media means accepting all kinds of inputs.

Questions, Questions and more Questions

Questions are bound to arise and you have to ask those questions if you want to succeed in your social media campaign. What are these fresh set of questions you may ask?

The first and foremost question which you have to ask is about your objectives. People expect either too much or too little for their efforts and that's a huge problem. Sometimes your business objectives just don't relate to your social media efforts. Living in such a situation causes more confusion. You must align your business goals with your social engagements. You should avoid platforms which are unsuitable – just don't rush into doing Pinterest because someone praised it. Have a holistic view.

Connecting the dotted line between your business goals and what social media wants to hear is critical. How can you make your audience listen to you? What stories can you generate which will keep your social media campaign fueled? The ultimate question you have to ask is whether you are listening to your customers. People will respond only when you listen and respond to them.

Social media is about building relationships. You can never be sure about what will eventually work and what won't. Have you ever asked why your competitor has succeeded or failed? In social media marketing, your competitor is your friend. You can learn a lot more from their success or failure than from personal experience.

One of the questions which we often fail to ask is this – How do you know you have succeeded or failed? How can you be sure about your social media marketing strategy? Having created content how can you ensure that it fits in well with your audience?

Sometimes we get carried away by the fact that social media marketing costs are low or negligible. This is a mistake. The time you spend on your marketing campaigns is precious. There are opportunity costs which you cannot even estimate. Unless you target the right audience and interact with them on the right platforms, you will be staring at disappointments. On the other hand, if you do the right things at the right time, you will succeed.

Your competitor is your best friend. Before you begin your social media journey, you should look at what your nearest competitor is doing. Have a look at their website. Do they have newsletters? How do they interact with their customers? How is the look and feel of their website? More importantly, observe how their customers respond. Look at the comments section carefully. This will provide you with significant inputs to improve your own site.

How do your competitors tell their story? Do they have a story at all? Fill in the gaps where you feel your competitor can do better. You will find opportunities which can give you an edge. Remember that the online market is huge. There is enough space for all the players. You can find your own niche within the market segment. There is no dearth of customers.

After examining your competitors, you will be in a position to develop your content strategy. Creating a content calendar is a great beginning. You can plan month on month. You must not think beyond a quarter because online scenarios have a tendency to change quickly. The trick is in learning and adapting. Never be rigid. Think laterally and freely. Don't get tied down by rules. There are no rules in social media marketing.

Frequently asked questions

There is no better place than the FAQ page to address your audience. You must be creative in your questions and cover the entire gamut of operations. Never leave any question unanswered. Customer queries are a great source of content. Tap your customers to find relevant questions.

Static means boring

Let's face it. Even the best content becomes stale over a period of time. Today's customers crave change – fast and furious change. They want action. They have an insatiable appetite. What do you do in such a situation? There are many ways to keep your customer hooked to your content.

Promotions and freebies are one of the best ways to sustain excitement. Buy one get one free is a time-tested formula. Remember to keep these promotions short and sweet. Create an artificial urgency. 'If you don't join the contest toady, you will never get another opportunity'. 'Last day for gala sales'. You can go on and on. If you protract your campaigns too long, you will find the excitement tapering off.

Online contests are a great way to encourage participations. You can ask your audience to create logos and short videos. You get multiple benefits from such contests. You get a copywriter free of cost and in return, you gift them your own product. Make sure that your contests are genuine and the winners are applauded in public. Ratchet up the excitement and let it peak dramatically. Promoting your customers is like promoting yourself – surrogate promotion.

What's important is participation. The more the contestants, the more the excitement.

Rebates and seasonal discounts are traditional marketing themes. They also work for online marketing. It is human nature to hanker for freebies and rebates. Why do you think discounts are so popular in a retail environment? You can even sell a sledge to an Eskimo in California, as long as your scheme is attractive enough. What about the loss of revenue? You can make up the losses by the quantity of sales and minor losses must be treated as marketing expenses. You will attract a huge audience and you can always tap them in future. These schemes will ensure that you have followers who can be targeted by you.

The last pair of shoes

Salespeople know the art of creating scarcity. 'This is the last pair of shoes. Buy now or you will regret later', is a trick which never fails. Use it to the hilt. Some businesses think that creating artificial scarcity is like duping the customers. Agreed that there is a thin line between fooling your customers and cajoling them. It is a well-known fact in psychology that people will only buy when they are pushed to do so. Customers need a reason to buy or they will postpone taking a decision. If someone believes that he or she will not get another opportunity, they will be compelled to take action. Seasonal sales give you an opportunity to push sales by positioning your schemes attractively.

Chapter 3 – Understanding Social Media

1. Understanding Twitter
2. Understanding Facebook
3. Linkedin, Tumbler, Pinterest, Google +

Understanding Twitter

Twitter literally means 'Make high-pitched sounds, as of birds'. Obviously, the Twitter application means just that. Not a long and winding lecture but a short hyphenated call to action. Someone has well said that brevity is the soul of wit. Twitter is all of 140 characters – thank heaven that at least in some things size doesn't matter.

On the flip side, many of us wonder how we can put our glorious thoughts in such a small packet and even if we can why it should make a difference. Initially, it did look as if it was a passing fad, like kids trying out some outlandish stuff and discarding it for another new toy in town. Even the most far-thinking fellows described it as a pastime for friends to keep each other informed. But over the years Twitter has transformed from an ugly little toy to a great beast of business. Marketing gurus now vouch for the efficacy of Twitter and swear by it. World leaders are tweeting. American President Donald Trump used Twitter to get heard during his election campaign. Even now he tweets regularly to keep in touch with his followers. Barrack Obama, Indian Prime Minister Narendra Modi are all Twitter addicts. They've more than 10 million followers and their single tweet can create waves throughout the world. These 140 characters have the power to even bring down a government. Film stars, businessmen, and celebrities are all on Twitter. Anybody can join Twitter as it is free.

So, what is Twitter?

It is an online application which helps people communicates with each other using maximum of 140 characters. When a person communicates or tweets, the message is instantaneously sent to many thousands of followers. We are talking about real time here. Recently, a bridegroom announced his wedding by tweeting right from the alter and just before exchanging wedding vows. Wonder what the bride must be thinking. But the tweeting made some waves worldwide.

It all started with some banal thoughts being tweeted like – I had breakfast just now. Or worse – Went to the loo. But let me assure you that all technological advances either began at some lab as part of some geek's pet theory or were part of some freak experiment. It is not surprising that Twitter was not considered as a serious marketing weapon till recently. Actually, Twitter can make you a millionaire. No exaggeration here. If done right, you can rake in a lot of serious cash using Twitter. As affiliates, to promote products, help websites get higher search ranking, to popularize blogs and you can do lots more with Twitter.

There can be no better tool than Twitter to amass a fan following in your niche. Remember that the world is your audience here. You can reach the tip of Iceland and the jungles of Amazon with Twitter instantaneously. By joining some websites which I have discussed earlier, you can populate your niche with Twitter followers. Because you have a passion for your particular niche, the enthusiasm and energy would automatically get passed on through your message. The response would also be equally enthusiastic, leading to a viral loop.

The Dell story

Dell computer uses Twitter to drive up their sales. The company reported that in two years of being on Twitter their sales went up by 34%. They made a cool $2 million thanks to Twitter. How did they do it? Here's the story - Dell has multiple accounts and reaches out to a million followers on Twitter. When one Tweet is placed in one of their accounts it is re-tweeted by the other accounts. This way they reach out to a wider audience. Instead of bombarding customers with a series of tweets Dell offered general news and customer service through Twitter. That helped them to interact with customers which in turn aided in jacking up their sales.

The four important aspects of Twitter marketing are engagement, promotions, retweets and retention. Dell was careful not to spam their customers. Else they would've been '*unfollowed*'. They only made their customers aware of what was happening in their business.

Having contests on Twitter will help to increase followers. Offer discounts and free stuff for referrals. That'll get you more followers and visibility. When domain provider *Namecheap* held a contest on Twitter and offered free domain registration to the first 100 early birds; their followers increased from 200 to 4000. They saw a 20% increase in sales too.

Airlines target their audience to keep them informed about flight delays and other happenings. A Tweet is a better way to inform all passengers rather than SMS. It is interesting to note that many shoppers spent more money on Twitter than Google this holiday season.

You can sell anything through Twitter. All you need is a smartphone and free account. Choose the name carefully for your account. Let it be something that'll remind people about your product. Twitter comes up with new and improved tools to promote products and businesses on their platform. Update yourself regularly. Also post at least twice in a week. Use Bitly to shorten your website address and share it on your Twitter page.

Re-tweet and keep adding followers regularly. Use Twitter's geo-positioning tool to search for people in your area and neighborhood. If your business is global then you can choose people around the world to follow you. Improve customer service and interact with people on a regular basis. Sometimes the messages are too many and you get overwhelmed. This is called information overload. Try to maximize your interaction with your followers.

You should link your website to all your social media accounts. Besides Twitter, you can also cross-sell through Facebook, Instagram and Google + and others. When you post a product on Twitter and advertise on other platforms as well then you're sure to drive traffic to your website.

Twitter also offers money per tweet from businesses. It's not that only celebrities are highly paid to re-tweet. Even an average person can earn $10 per tweet. In a case where your fan base is more than 50,000, then you'll be lucky to get up to $100. That depends on how you engage your followers and how powerful your advertising pitch is for the product. This can be a second income where you get extra cash to buy that designer dress you saw on social media.

Call to action

Remember that a tweet is a message – all activities must be coordinated towards that one tweet. Focus, focus, and focus! Never lose sight of your business. Some tweets may elicit laughter, some may be deeply spiritual and others may move you to tears. We have different goals. We are here to make money and a fortune. Every tweet must, therefore, give a clear message. Leave the fun and games to others. Your tweets must be impactful, dynamic and each one must have a call to action. By this I mean you must compel your followers to do more than just follow. 'Visit mysite.com', or 'More at mysite.com' are some examples of call to action. If humor can be incorporated you are welcome, but simply eliciting laughter is not your goal.

Twitter is an amazing tool that is hands-on, realistic, wide-ranging and extremely effective for gaining stunning results.

Understanding Facebook

When a few lady homemakers from Detroit who were good at knitting, crocheting, painting and preparing delectable cookies came together they decided to monetize their skills. Though they had their own day jobs as school teachers and boutique manager, etc they felt that extra income is always welcome. But they didn't know how to showcase their talent as there was no way they could open a shop or gallery. All that cost money, and moreover, they were in no position to invest their precious time. After all, they had their jobs. That is when they decided to open a page on Facebook and post pictures of their products. They were thrilled to know that it's free to have a page on Facebook. They named their page 'ladypreneurs' as they were women who were entrepreneurs. They posted their handiworks and shared them on their personal timeline as well. They requested their friends to 'like' the page and become a member. Each one of them had more than 1000 friends (approx) on

Facebook. Within a week ladypreneurs had 10,000 members and there was a lot of conversation going on about the paintings and crochet apparels. This encouraged the women to approach Facebook to market their page. The Facebook marketing team was very happy to help and for a meager $90 per month 'ladypreneurs' was marketed on Facebook. It is important here to say that Facebook acted as their window display shop for free. There was no need for a shop, paying rental & electricity bills, having workers and decorating the shop. All these expenses were done away thanks to Facebook.

Facebook placed the page link on the home pages of all the 10,000 members. Each member had more than 500 friends and it was a huge customer base to start with. Once the queries started coming in the ladies asked their clients to make payment through PayPal and the products were delivered to their doorstep. Initially, it was a simple arrangement. It was the next step that was surprising. More ladies wanted to join ladypreneurs to sell their products. One woman from New Jersey wanted to sell her imitation jewelry whereas another from San Jose wanted to sell clothes. A third wanted to advertise aromatic candles and this way ladypreneurs got not only customers but sellers as well.

Facebook facilitated these ladypreneurs to have geo-targeted pages all across America and that helped them to showcase their products. Today ladypreneurs has gone worldwide and women are able to buy and sell products thanks to Facebook. These women have been able to not only showcase their talent but have managed to have a secondary income thanks to Facebook. In fact, a few of the women have even quit their day job and made this their primary income. They're able to grow their customer base and have their own website to sell their products. Some have employed workers and marketing professionals also.

Facebook is an amazing social media platform where there are more than a billion people having their profiles. If your product is global like say a software where it is only a download then the whole world is there waiting for you. All you need is zest and zeal to push forward and make a sale.

When Facebook started out it was just a photo sharing site where friends and relatives could connect with each other. Since it is free to join everybody has a profile on Facebook. It won't be an exaggeration to say that the entire country is on Facebook. Make one post and put it on your timeline and tag your friends. If your post is interesting then you'll see many people have shared it. Sharing makes it go viral.

How to get customers through Facebook?

When you make an advert, Facebook asks you to target the age group of the audience, their place of stay and sex. Accordingly, they place the ads on the right side of those profiles. Facebook analyzes your profile to see your feeds, the pages you and your friends like as well as your profile. They share your phone number and email address with the business and they add it to their customer list. They also connect through your IP address, your location through GPS and setting up of your Facebook and Instagram profile.

When Citi Bank wanted more credit card applicants they used Facebook adverts to collect more leads. Businesses today are depending on social media to promote their products as the cost is negligible. Print and television commercials cost a lot. Whereas a simple advert in social media for a pittance can make your product visible to the whole world. For example, an artist who's showcasing his painting from New Jersey can sell it to a customer in Nebraska. There is no limit for your audience.

Facebook marketing team helps you to advertise as well as manage your page on a daily basis. You can choose the amount you wish to pay for your advert. You can fix the daily budget as well as annual budget. It's flexible and easy to use. In case you wish to stop the promotion of your product, go to the 'manage my account page' and remove your advert.

You're in control of your ad budget. There are three things you need to take into account before you spend on ads;

1. The size of the audience,

2. Time schedule of the ad

3. Your bid to reach your audience.

Once the ad starts to appear on the right side of the profiles you only pay if someone 'clicks' on them and reaches your page. There are two aspects to your billing methods. Budget and spend. Budget is the amount you set aside for the ad and the spend is how much you've actually spent. For example – say you have a budget of $100 but only $60 is spent because the clicks were only for that amount then your budget is $100 whereas your spend is $60. There is also a daily budget and lifetime budget for the ads. In case you wish to know more about Facebook billing methods, go here-

https://www.facebook.com/business/help/494368557244384/?helpref=hc_fnav

Ten years ago Facebook was at its nascent stage. The founder didn't know how to monetize it. The investors were looking at IPO (public issue) to exit the company. But the IPO was a damp squib and Facebook was in the red. Thanks to entrepreneurs like Varun Agarwal who used Facebook to advertise and sell his Tshirts with the school's logo, Facebook realized their strength and started taking advertisements. Slowly they auctioned advert space and today have reached a comfortable space. It is tipped that they'll have a net income of $10billion by end 2017.

That is the power of social media. Whether it is Facebook, Twitter, Instagram or any other space they are all looking at humongous figures as their user base is expanding rapidly. LinkedIn, Google +, Tumblr and Pinterest are other mediums that can also help to market businesses.

Monetize your business using Linkedin, Tumbler, Pinterest, Google +

Time and again, studies have shown that people who follow their heart are the most successful in life and business alike. When was the last time you jumped out of bed with sheer excitement? Was this because you were passionate about your work and business? There used to be a time when successful people talked about the fire in their belly. Successful people still talk about it but the message is lost in the jungle of PPC, SEO, affiliate, the internet and so on..........Don't simply look around what people are doing and try to copy them. Originals are way more precious than copies. All of us are passionate about something. We are naturally good in doing specific tasks. You may be a good artist, singer or possibly you appreciate art and antiques. I mean you could be good at anything and that must become your niche. If you are groaning and cussing daily after getting out of bed, you are simply not doing the right thing.

Even with the most sincere efforts, many don't taste success. Some call it destiny or fate and resign themselves to the fact that they are not as successful as they would like to be. But modern technology gives ample opportunity for everyone to succeed. Here are some things you ought to do:

Google +

Google search has created magic and transformed the way we work, play and become rich. Having identified your niche (using your internal compass), you type in the word/words you are interested in. You will get thousands of results, which must be analyzed. Does this niche have enough following? If yes, your work is cut out. Following some simple techniques, which were discussed in the earlier chapter, you can create a decent list of clientele. If your niche doesn't seem to be attracting many visitors, you must use this as an opportunity to create a compelling story which attracts people and persuades them to buy into it. In fact, if the niche you are looking for is still unexplored, I will call it a true niche. I have known guys who have become dejected and forlorn after finding that their particular niche was not so popular. Whenever I see this, I point out to them that they had actually stumbled on a gold mine. It only required a little spade work and the money would come pouring in. There was a particular instance where an amateur antique watch repairer, made a fortune.

Google + is an amazing social media platform that connects you with like-minded people. You just need to key in the right words and your profile is likely to get friends from your fraternity. The advantage of Google + is your email is linked and so is your search page. Google+ takes all this into account and throws up the right audience for you. Though it is not all that popular like Facebook it has its own niche audience. Google + boasts that they've 250 million users and out of that amount, 50% log in every day. When you're promoting your business it is better to be seen and heard on all social media platforms.

Include keywords and relevant links on your About page. This will explain your business to your audience. You can link back to specific pages on your website from your About page. Make sure that your website pages are SEO friendly. Get Authorship. It's the best way to get your picture next to your listings in search results. Google authenticates you through Authorship and will begin to trust you as a quality source of content. It is very simple to get Authorship. This will throw up your profile on search results resulting in higher ranking and click through rates.

Social sites like Google +, Tumblr and Pinterest are excellent breeding grounds for finding and nurturing your niche. Sometimes your imagination stops at the most popular social sites and you tend to ignore some niche websites. A bit of research can lead to some fantastic new discoveries. Ignorance can be a bliss but in some cases, it also means lost opportunities. Try and find sites that are into your niche/ market.

Tips and tricks to stay ahead of competition

As mentioned earlier, the best way to deal with competition is not to have any. If your niche is truly a niche you should not worry about competition. Mostly, what people call a niche is nothing but a huge opportunity which others have already exploited threadbare. Probably these niches have had their day under the sun but they can no longer be termed as a niche- they are mainstream businesses.

Play the spy game

The competition will always be there. If there is honey there will be bees. This is the truth. But competitors can be a wonderful source of information. This is a time-tested method – to spy on the competition. Businesses have been doing this for ages. It has become all the easier in this internet era. Join as a member in your competitor's forum. Become their follower on social media. By doing this you will remain one step ahead of the competition. Your competitors will be doing just this. Be careful when you divulge your future plans. Business savvy is as important today as earlier. This game should be played smartly.

Unique proposition

USP or unique selling proposition, means you offer something different, more or unique to your customers. Offer exclusive solutions, provide add-ons and give out attractive prizes. Keep your customers involved and guessing. Interact with them at regular intervals. Your business should always be buzzing with the latest information and solutions. Do you offer... Incentives to your regular customers? Do you have a loyalty program? How do you say thanks to your customers? Why should your customer remain a customer? I am sure you have not analyzed your business from this perspective. There cannot be a better way to win than by winning your customer's heart.

LinkedIn

LinkedIn is a social media platform where there are professionals, job seekers and experts from every field. Unlike other social media platforms like Facebook and Twitter where you're directly in touch with customers, LinkedIn offers business to business connections. It is a serious platform where you can create visibility for your product. Having a LinkedIn account will help to authenticate you and your business. Moreover, the people you're linked to can also vouch for your reputation.

LinkedIn helps you to create contacts, generate leads and find partners and also creating awareness for your brand. When you create contacts, you should send personal messages thanking them for connecting with you. This will establish your status. Make them a part of your email marketing list. You're only allowed to link 50 people at a time. You can add as many connections as you want over a period of time. Offer them a joining bonus or gift in the email. Make it personal. That'll help you to garner more support for your product.

Create a killer profile

You need to think things through before you create a profile. Address your business goals and let the people know more about your product and its specifications. Don't make a sales pitch. LinkedIn users are professionals. Describe your company's goal and aim. That'll help you to market your product. Besides your profile, post articles on your profile page. That'll help your viewers to understand you as a person. LinkedIn gives visibility to thousands of consultants, mentors, financial investors, students, innovators, etc. Life coach, counselors can also market themselves here. If you've written a book, promote it here. Post the link and reviews for people to see.

As an employer, ask all your employees to join LinkedIn and create a group. Keep your flock together; let them 'share' your posts. That'll help a lot in making your posts go viral.

Link with everyone in the industry

A sponsored update is a brilliant technique to endorse content that is helpful to the targeted audience. This gives out a strong call to action. People don't want to see pure advertising anymore and want something useful for free. By promoting your company's content through a LinkedIn sponsored update, your company can aim at your niche market to boost footfalls to your website. Depending upon the content's impact you can even get some sales conversions.

Go Viral

Posting an article directly on LinkedIn will enable your links to read the article and rate it with a 'like' as well as comments down below. If you have more than 100 readers, LinkedIn will put a spotlight on their main page. This will enable your post to reach more than tens of thousands of readers. Your profile will gain visitors and that is how more people will follow you. You can also make an announcement about your next post.

Join target groups

Create your own LinkedIn group. Keep your members together and join other groups. Look for prospective customers in those groups. Once you find a few ask them to join your group. Give them some incentive. This will enable you to keep all your prospective customers in one group. Don't allow rival competitors to enter your group. Check out every individual's profile before you accept them into your group. Poach your prospects and keep them together. This is a grand way to promote your business and build leads.

Connect with Twitter

Connect your twitter account to your LinkedIn profile. It is observed that whatever you post in your twitter feed has interaction on your LinkedIn profile. When people talk about your update it stays on the top of their mind for a while.

Update regularly / be active

Update regularly. Keep aside half an hour each day to browse through social media. Be active and respond to comments as well as criticism. Sometimes negative comments from a disgruntled person will attract more attention and give you mileage. You should respond in a matured way to those negative comments. That will propel your post to be 'shared' and commented by your 'friends' and this will help you to get noticed.

When Marcus, a start-up consultant joined LinkedIn he had only 50 followers. He wrote a post about how startups had to pitch their businesses to Venture Capitalists in just three minutes. That post received a lot of 'comments'. He had made fun of the VC's and wondered how a start-up can actually make a pitch in 3 minutes. After all, large amounts of money are getting pumped in. That irked one of his followers (who was a VC) and he commented that Marcus is indeed out of his mind. A couple of Marcus's followers who were start up guys supported Marcus and the post was shared by more than 3000 people within three hours. LinkedIn too promoted it seeing the heavy traffic for this particular post. Marcus received 1000 follow requests and he gladly accepted all of them. He made the title of his posts attractive and controversial; that attracted readers. Out of the 1000 follow requests most of them were university students waiting to start their own company and were looking for funding and mentors. Marcus advised them on how to start small and became a mentor to a few of them. In a year's time, two of them received 3 million dollars funding and took off on their own.

Marcus got a percentage of shares from the company and moved on to help other start-ups. He proudly put it on display in all his social media handles about his achievements and more people became 'friends' requesting him to help them.

Tumblr

Tumblr is a micro-blogging and social networking site where the teenagers of America are raring to be. Found in 2007 by David Karp it is now purchased by Yahoo. They boast about a 350 million users and their revenue has touched $1 billion. Tumblr lets you share anything and everything. Re-sharing/ re-blogging is the most popular form on Tumbler. Be it text, blog post or music video or audio, photos, quotes, links, etc anything and everything can be shared on Tumblr. Another way to optimize is by 'tagging'. You can tag your posts with keywords specific to your niche so that your post shows up when someone is searching your niche. Their user interface is smooth and allows excellent navigation. It is interesting to note that most of its content is only re-sharing and not original. Still, they boast a wide audience as 60% of them are teenagers. Tumblr is the best platform to advertise for native crowdsourced advertising.

The best part of using Tumblr is it makes any medium feel native. You can be an individual promoting your products or expertise like a musician or a company selling goods; all have their own space here for promotion. You can join your niche community so that it'll be easy to target your audience. The 'my dashboard' is custom made for you depending on the people you follow. The uniqueness of Tumblr is it'll only connect you to blogs and people whom you are interested in and not like Facebook where unwanted people's profiles are also thrown on your home page. Tumblr allows you to directly message people.

Since Tumbler's main audience is teenagers; bands, musicians, dance videos, artists, and models are promoting themselves here. They have a large audience and followers have become popular here. Tumblr also offers paid URL's without the tag Tumblr. It is customized to suit you. You can have your own web page to promote yourself as well as your products. Your target audience will get updates about you on their dashboard and they can visit your page to have a look at your offers.

Calvin Klien, the famous American fashion house promotes his products through Tumblr and has made killer sales during the holiday seasons.

Pinterest

With 100 million followers Pinterest is the best way to market your business. Started in 2010 in San Francisco it's very easy and free to open a Pinterest account. Once you reach their site and sign up using your email, and 'click' the request invite button, Pinterest will send you an invite.

Register and post pictures. You can also pin another person's post or picture on your profile. Pinterest is basically a personal media platform wherein you can promote yourself. Their 'pin' is similar to share on Facebook and re-tweet on Twitter. Not only can you promote your products you can also become an affiliate and promote other's products. For example, you can become an affiliate on Amazon and start promoting the book on Pinterest. Embed the link and pin it.

Start a free blog through Word Press or BlogSpot. Unless you have a blog or a website, your social media accounts alone will not help. Pin your blog URL here. In case you have an 'opt in' page or 'subscribe' page, take a screenshot and pin it here. If you're offering any freebies or discounts make an attractive image and pin it. That'll appeal to your followers. The images you use should be striking and gorgeous. Search keywords on Pinterest for 'sign up' and 'join our mailing list'. You'll get an idea of what others are doing.

Have a video wherein you explain in detail about your product or niche. Pin it back to your sales page so that people learn more about the product. Also, create images of customer testimonials. Let them be in quote form. That'll speak for your capabilities. Share small tips to keep the customer interested in you. Be it a dish to cook or a new dress to buy or a place to visit; all tips are available on Pinterest. It is a visual bookmarking tool that has been a favorite among women to help and save creative ideas.

Chapter 4 - 6 Google Marketing Tools You Should Be Using

Google has transformed the way we use the internet. There was a time in the late 90's when you had to type the correct web address to reach a website. With the advent of Google, everything changed. You just need to type a few words into the search algorithm through various websites using the same keywords. Keyword search became the key to online marketing. SEO (Search Engine Optimization) is the new phenomenon of the 21st century. The world has shrunk and within seconds you can access anything anywhere in the world.

More than 1.17 billion users search on Google. The user base is massive and it is only prudent for any business to use Google marketing tools. Here are some of the tools that are essential to market your products on Google.

1. Google My Business
2. Google + Business pages

3. Google Adwords
4. Google keyword Planner
5. Google Trends
6. PPC – pay per click marketing

1) Google My Business

Formerly known as Google Places, Google My business is very popular among local area advertisers. For example, if you're running a restaurant then get listed on Google My Business. Use keywords like restaurant, Dallas, Mexican, burrito, etc on your website. When someone in Dallas is looking for Mexican food and searches Google your website and listing will appear to him. In fact, Google Maps will also show the way to your restaurant and how much time it'll take to reach.

2) Google+ Business Pages

It is critical to have a Google + page for your business. With your 'my business' listing it is ideal to link your Google + page to your website and my business. Since Google is a gigantic domain it's better to have your local business set up on Google +. It is free so you don't lose anything.

3) Google AdWords

One of the basic advantages of using Google AdWords is simply the span of its reach. It may be a surprise to many of you to know that AdWords has a directory of over 10 billion web pages and over 100 different language versions! The size and reach of Google AdWords offer certain unique benefits that you wouldn't be able to get on other PPC Search Engines. For instance, using AdWords increases your exposure (even if your site already appears in Google's organic search results) by listing your site prominently in its own as well as its related search networks.

For sophisticated users – those among you who have already experienced internet advertisers and high up on the PPC Search Engine learning curve – Google provides a long and comprehensive list of options and useful tools. You'd be surprised (if you're not already aware) that such options and tools include, among others, local search with advanced mapping via Google Earth; day-parting; geo-targeting; site targeting; site map generation; choice of contextual advertising; free Google Analytics etc. The Google Analytics, which is integrated with AdWords, helps you to evaluate which keywords are performing well and which you should consider dropping. Similarly, a Website Optimizer enables you to work on alternative versions of landing page marketing content to ascertain which version has a better probability of conversion.

Flexibility is another advantage in AdWords. You can edit your Ads; modify text and the copy; choose text or image Ads to suit your product/marketing needs; target your Ads to specific geographical locations, and even choose the language you want to advertise in. You can make these changes continuously until you achieve the desired results.

You can simultaneously create and run as many Ad campaigns as you want; build them up against separate keyword clusters, and bid on as many key phrases as your budget allows. This you'd agree is as flexible as 'flexible' can get!

How Adwords works

You must have by now got a fair idea of what AdWords is all about, but probably need more substantial information to be able to sign up and work with the program.

AdWords is Google's text-based system for you to advertise your products or services on its own as well as its partners' sites. It's a flexible service which allows you to create your own Ads; choose and modify keywords to align your Ads to the needs of your audience, and advertise your products in an economical way – you pay Google only when people click on your Ad (a Cost-Per-Click arrangement). It is also easy to enroll in the AdWords program.

The concept of AdWords is quite simple: You have a product which you want to market to people who are actually interested in the product category and are, in fact, already on the lookout/searching for a suitable offer. You create Ads using suitable keywords to suit your product. AdWords sells you ad space which shows up alongside the Google search results (in the 'Sponsored Links' column on the right or the top of the page) when somebody searches for such specific terms (keywords). People can simply click on your Ad to make a purchase or know more about you depending on how you have designed the Ad.

For example, if you have a site for selling an online dictionary, you might want your Ad to appear when people search for *online dictionary* or *internet dictionary* or *electronic dictionary* and so on. The Ad will appear depending on the quality and relevancy (to the visitor's search item) that you have been able to incorporate in your Ad. But remember that you will not be charged when your Ad is displayed – you will be charged *only* if somebody clicks on your Ad.

At this stage, it may be worthwhile to take some time off to consider how your Cost-Per–Click will be set and how much you'd be charged per click. You need to know this (and your sales conversion rate) to not only set your PPC Ad budget but also to understand whether you are making money at all from your ad campaign or simply losing money from every sales transaction (conversion) that occurs.

Since your actual CPC reduces when the Quality score of your Ad increases, you should have a fair idea of how Ad ranking is done by the PPC

Search Engine industry. Note the words *'fair idea'*. In many cases, and particularly with Google AdWords, the actual methodology for ranking (assigning Quality Score in the case of Google) and pricing of Ads is a closely guarded company secret. As far as AdWords is concerned, while the broad parameters for computing the Quality Score have been defined by Google, such as CTR, historical performance of keywords, the relevance of Ad text, and quality of the Ad's landing page; not much has been divulged about the actual method of calculating the Quality Score. One can therefore only surmise on the individual sub-components and the weights assigned to each of them in deriving the final score (and ranking). At this time, suffice it to say that the Click-Through-Rate of your Ad is a significant driver for raising your Quality Score.

It is clear from the above that you have two options to raise your Ad ranking; raise your maximum bid price (remember that you have the flexibility to do this at any time) or try and improve the Quality Score of your Ad. The first option raises your cost and, if not used prudently, will likely put you into the red. The second option does not raise your cost (in fact it reduces the cost!) while raising your Ad's slot in the Sponsored Links box.

While on the subject of costs, you should also know that like the actual calculation of the Quality Score by Google (which is unclear), the methodology applied by Google for determining your CPC is also a somewhat gray area. With AdWords, the price you pay per click is related (though exactly how is not revealed by Google) to the Quality Score and rank obtained by your Ad. A higher Quality Score for your Ad ensures that you may not actually be paying as much as your maximum bid price (though you may be charged more than the charges for similar Ads ranked higher). The monitoring of your Ad quality by Google is a dynamic process and the Quality Score (QS) will fluctuate; an increase automatically triggering a reduction in the CPC and vice versa. This means that the higher your QS, the lower is the price you will pay when someone clicks on your Ad.

You can appreciate from all that has been discussed so far, that the best way to sustain a cost-effective Pay-Per-Click campaign on AdWords is to ensure that you are able to maintain a high-Quality Score for your Ad continuously. You can do this by keeping a close watch on your AdWord account statistics (keyword status, CTR and minimum bid etc) so that you can make changes as necessary.

4) Google AdWords Keyword Planner

The keyword planner helps you to identify highly searched keywords for your niche so that you can create blog content accordingly. You can optimize your web content so that you focus on SEO to be found during the organic search. You can also look for new keyword ideas, and keyword planner helps you to do just that. To use keyword planner you first need to have an Adwords account.

5) Google Trends

As the name suggests this tool enables you to find about the latest happenings and Google search criteria changes. It'll help you to make smart keyword choices. You can assess the popularity of keywords and phrases so that you have an idea to create your content accordingly. Another major advantage of Google Trends is it is available in different languages and shows you the region's trends and suggestions. Whenever you're in a dilemma of which keyword to choose for your blog title, consult Google Trends to know exactly what works. Trends keeps you updated on latest news, happenings and local information of your area almost real time.

6) PPC - Pay-Per-Click

PPC, simply put, is the placement of an Ad on a search engine results page or a web page (termed a 'Landing page') that is extracted or appears for specified keywords or key phrases. Whenever a visitor who has 'landed' on that page clicks on the Ad that you have put there, the advertiser pays a pre-determined price (or bid amount). As an advertiser, you pay *only* if a visitor clicks on your Ad on the website. This is why this system is called 'Pay-Per-Click'.

The number (or volume) of targeted quality visitors to the specified website (and Ad) makes up the Pay-Per-Click Traffic. The trick of the trade is to be able to promote the product well enough (possibly through PPC campaigns) to ensure that you convert as much of the traffic, as possible, into sales.

The Pay-Per-Click traffic has become very popular as a promotional tool in internet marketing, with both vendors and affiliates. PPC traffic is increasing very fast.

One reason, no doubt, is the ever-expanding reach of the internet; the other, and main, being the advantages the system provides, in terms of speed, flexibility, and economy, to vendors, affiliates and website sponsors (say, for instance, Google).

The advantage of speed, mentioned above, can be gauged from the fact that PPC Ads can appear within a short span of two days after application to the PPC search engine (and in some cases within minutes!) The aim of PPC search engine marketing is to drive targeted traffic to your website; and it does so promptly and efficiently if properly used. This is one of the main reasons for its popularity, particularly in affiliate marketing.

PPC Search Engines normally rank sponsored Ads from top to bottom of the 'Sponsored Links' box. Google AdWords also follows this system and higher ranked Ads find a higher slot on the 'Sponsored Links' box. The higher up the 'Sponsored Links' box your Ad is, the more traffic and 'clicks' it's likely to get. Google AdWords also rewards higher ranked Ads by charging a lesser price. Your effort, therefore, should be for your Ads to stay as near the top as possible and at the same time, at a reasonable cost!

There are, literally, hundreds of Pay-Per-Click Search Engines you can buy traffic from on the web. The search engines differ in terms of volume of traffic, quality of traffic, audience reach, cost-effectiveness for a higher Return on Investment (ROI) (start-up costs, bid prices, minimum bid price etc), safety features (fraud detection/ protection), search innovations, customer support, and services etc. As their number increases, it becomes more and more difficult to determine which one is the best for you. And may heaven help you if you are a beginner!

Chapter 5 - Video/ YouTube Marketing

Marques Brownlee is a 24-year-old African American tech video blogger whose videos are popular on YouTube. He works under the name MKBHD. He grew up in a small neighborhood in New Jersey and had a penchant for anything tech right from a teenager. As a high school student, he started uploading reviews about tech gadgets as a hobby. His interest in hardware made him an expert among friends and peers. He reviewed all the latest products that came into the market and also demonstrated how people can use them. Initially, he just posted pictures of the product and talked about them. He also responded to viewers through text. This interaction made him popular among viewers. As his viewership increased tech companies approached him to promote their products for a fee. Marques, who was in college at the time, agreed, and later became a full-time YouTuber sharing his opinions on his tech platform.

As time passed, Marques completed his bachelor's degree and his viewer base increased tenfold and touched a million a couple of years ago. That is when Marques decided to add video broadcasting of the products in detail and moved away from pictures to live streaming of the products. He had a deep knowledge about the products and what his viewers wished to know about them. His famous videos are about I-phones and his views are taken seriously by his viewers as well as the companies. Two years ago he reviewed I-phone 6's scratch test of the front glass display. That particular video went viral and the top magazines like Huffington Post and Time, amongst others, featured it. Marques got approximately 8 million views for that single video.

Today Marques has more than 4.5 million subscribers and the number is growing by the day. All he does is give his honest opinion about a product to consumers as phones and tech gadgets are the most popular purchases people do today. He's also featured on television channels and talk shows.

Marques earn around $750 per day and his income is pegged at $300,000 only through advertising. Besides he also earns through promotions and product reviews. People throng his tech channel as he loves what he does. He is serious, diligent and passionate about his work and his opinions are well respected. Marques reviews out of a passion for gadgets and not for money. The beauty of YouTube is, he just uploads the videos and Google do all the back-end work for him.

There are many success stories like Marques on YouTube. Be it electronic gadgets; makeup tutorials, cookery or apparels, all are advertised on YouTube. This medium has become very powerful and it's absolutely free to upload videos. You can also promote them through your Facebook and Twitter handles. Even businesses are resorting to video marketing where you can showcase your products. The script for the video should be entertaining with light humor. Don't make it too serious. At the end of each video have a *'click to subscribe button'*. This pushes the people to subscribe to your other videos as well. You don't need professional equipment to shoot videos; a simple camera will do. Hire a videographer and shoot the videos in your office. Viewers are more interested in your opinions and what is shown about the product than location. Your expense for video marketing will be negligible. Initially, you can do it yourself or ask a friend. Once you start seeing some money, go in for a videographer.

Phones, iPods, tablets, laptops and all other electronic products are advertised through YouTube. As said earlier, you just need to shoot and upload. Rest of the back end work is taken care by Google. You can promote your videos through your other social media accounts also. Besides, you can have a website and upload your videos there too.

How to measure success on YouTube?

Instead of depending only on views go a little deeper and see how many people have viewed the complete video. Are there any repeat views? What is the drop off rate? Dig deeper to analyze the data and track each and every individual viewer. Communicate with them to know their opinion. That'll not only establish your authenticity it'll help to build more views too.

Big companies such as Coca-Cola, Samsung, Toyota, Sony, and Disney are marketing on YouTube amongst many other consumer giants. Video content marketing needs emphasis here. Companies are investing huge amounts on video marketing. The ideal way to market is to upload the video both on YouTube and your website and link them together. There are YouTube graders available. Pixability is one such grader. They help you to analyze your search engine score, YouTube score, website score and social media score. This will give you an idea about the success of your video marketing. Engage with customers and that'll lead to more shares. More shares mean more visibility.

Like any other marketing strategy, research, plan and build a solid approach to your video marketing. Keep your focus, understand your audience, assess your competitors and decide how to place your content. Once you've all the keys in place build a robust video marketing strategy to achieve thumping success and continuous sales.

Musicians, teachers, tutors, hair stylist, beautician, chefs and gardeners, anybody and everybody can market through YouTube. An Australian horticulturist talks about how you can grow a vegetable garden at home and his videos show step by step about building a garden. He talks and shows how the compost is made and used, the seeds to be sowed and how to water the plants and incremental growth of the plants at every stage. The videos are interesting, informative and also attractive as he and his glamorous partner participate together in the video. His videos attract more than 100,000 views and his business has started growing as more and more people are trooping to his office to buy compost and seeds and saplings.

This only shows that whatever you may be selling, as long as you have the passion and sincerity, you can become the next YouTube sensation.

Chapter 6 - Integrate social media with your website

Two decades ago when websites came into existence, businesses still had to send out brochures and mailers to prospective clients to visit their website. These websites were static and offered information about the business. People visited the website, roamed around and then left never to return. Why do you think it happened? Business owners thought that their website wasn't attractive; the colors didn't match and revamped their site often. But the truth was it wasn't the look of the website but the content that mattered. Well, there was only content trying to sell their product and it wasn't compelling enough.

With the advent of blogs, websites grew less in importance as blogs were easy to maintain and integrate with the website. Slowly an RSS (really simple syndication) feed was added to the website. This made it easy for subscribers to get the relevant content you've added to your website. It intimated the subscribers when the fresh content was added and pulled them back to visit your website. So from being a static website your site became lively and began breathing. RSS keeps your current and prospective customers in touch with your business. This is a totally different paradigm than a brochure or newsletter.

With the arrival of social media like Facebook and twitter, businesses started to move towards them. They shared pictures of their products on their Facebook and gave links to their website. Interested people visited the website to look for more information. Then came YouTube where businesses uploaded videos about their products and businesses. They promoted it by sharing the links on their websites as well as on other social media platforms.

Button up your website

Add social media buttons prominently on your site. The buttons should be placed either on the top or bottom of the page. You can also put it on the side but see to it that it remains in your navigation as the visitor moves from one page to another. See to it that all your social media platforms are operational and active. Otherwise, remove the buttons that are not working. No point in your customer visiting your social media handle that is nonoperational.

You can also use cross promotion on your Facebook, Twitter and Instagram pages and provide a link to your website on all these platforms. Integrate all your promotional links along with your website on your email as well. Also, see to it that the buttons are latest and not a year old. Facebook has changed its button from F to thumbs up. So keep your social media buttons up to date as it adds to your credibility. In case you're running an E-Commerce site add a Share or Add This button on your pages. Else you'll be losing out on a whole lot of sales as readers will not be able to recommend your product. Pay attention to the way your social media accounts are being handled by readers and visitors. That'll give you an idea about how successful your products are or what you can do to promote them aggressively.

The major advantage of social media presence is your website will attract traffic and by having social media buttons on your website your social media pages will also get traffic from your site. So you see its double advantage to have a strong online presence for your business.

Monetize through Instagram

As the name signifies it is instant and gets viewed by people around the world as soon as you post a picture. Instagram stories are a popular way to promote your products. The Kardashian sisters make millions of dollars by promoting apparels, beauty products, shoes, and clothing. Each one of them has more than 5 million followers and one picture immediately reaches millions of users. Each of the Kardashian sister's earns more than $500,000 per annum just by promoting products on their Instagram account.

The best way to monetize on Instagram is to have multiple accounts. Have different emails for each account and integrate them so that you can cross-sell your products. Your account name should be attractive and suitable for your product. For example- if you're selling shoes your account name should signify it – Lace it up or Booty In, etc. See to it that the username is funky and trendy. Don't be old fashioned. Remember that modern people especially youngsters use Instagram. Your product should cater to the young audience. When you've multiple accounts you can make thousands of followers for each account. For example, if you've 7 accounts of ten to fifteen thousand followers per account then instantly you can reach an audience of 70,000 to 100,000 followers. Your product will gain visibility instantly with 100,000 people. As per modest marketing metrics at least 10% will become your customers and buy your product. With one Instagram post/story, you sell at least 10,000 products easily. That is the power of social media. They get you instant eyeballs and converts visitors into customers.

Link it up

Link your website to your Instagram account. That'll get you more conversions. Don't forget to add hashtags while promoting products. Customers are tired of looking for products online. There are billions of them. So give them an easy to use interface where the hashtag will bring them to your site. Online shopping can be made simpler by click through links.

Set up your Instagram profile

1. Create your account on Engage hub. *Engage Hub* is a technology company that provides mobile data-driven customer

engagement solutions. It is very easy. Choose a spontaneous name that suits your product. You can even add your Twitter and Facebook accounts to this.

2. Add the link to your profile. Reach the design section from where you can choose the color, look, and design of your page. Display your name or brand name, commercial button and source icon.
3. If it is powered by Shopify then it only takes a minute to add a page and put the HTML code on EngageHub.
4. Copy the embed code and put it in your page code. Now your Instagram page is ready for selling your products.
5. Post pictures or share images to sell. Use hashtags.

The ease of operation makes Engage Hub an attractive option. Customers need to only make a few clicks to buy from your Instagram page. By adding hash tag# campaigns you make it easy for the public to locate the product of their choice. This simplifies the navigation thereby increasing sales.

How to monetize your page?

Now that your account is ready to start marketing on Instagram as well as other social media outlets, send 'shout outs'. This will enable your product to be showcased on various pages. Shout outs are like re-tweeting on Twitter or sharing a post on Facebook. You simply share another person's product or your own from a different profile page.

There are more than 400 million registered users on Instagram. You have a whole wide world to showcase your products. There is a huge potential here. Go to [Instagram help](#) to set up your account. Learn everything about Instagram before you get started.

Earn through referrals

You can actually share others products on your page as an affiliate marketer to earn money on Instagram. You're paid to post products. If you've more than a million followers, sponsors and businesses would like to engage you. At the same time if out of a million followers only 300 like your posts then you're not suitable as a brand ambassador or affiliate. In case you have a few thousand followers yet your likes are higher, then sponsors may be interested in you.

Instead of simply sharing products on your profile, make custom written content for each of the product. That'll endear you to the sponsors.

Buy shout outs

It's very easy to buy shout outs on Instagram. If your product can appear on 1000 pages at a time then it'll be a big boost to your marketing efforts. Sales are likely to increase with shout outs. Shoutcart.com offers purchase of shout outs. The cost is negligible. Don't buy blindly as you're likely to be blocked or spammed. Choose the profiles that you think are suitable for your product. Buy them through Shoutcart to promote your products. Shoutcart has added the latest technique where your Twitter followers can also view your Instagram promotion. Use keyword search to find your niche audience. This is sure to increase traffic tenfold.

Use shopseen

Shopseen application is very easy to use. It turns your Instagram account into an online store. Link your Instagram profile to Shopseen and once it is confirmed start adding images of your products. You can also add in descriptions and prices. The buyer tracks through your profile link to make payments using credit cards on a protected server.

Use Yotpo's Shoppable Instagram

Yotpo's Shoppable Instagram feature not only links your page and keeps track of your products and sales; it also sends messages to customers when you post new updates. Shoppable links products that are tagged and directs followers to Shoppable feed via photo captions. The buyer can complete the purchase in the Shoppable feed. Shoppable also adds value by rating a product, giving buyer testimonies and letting you know how many products are sold, etc. This enables the buyer to take a decision. This is a unique feature that only Shoppable offers. Their conversion rate is high and bounce rate is low.

What do you need to create an Instagram account?

It's free to start an Instagram account. You can write an attractive bio and link your Instagram account to your Facebook profile as well as phone number. That'll provide authenticity and prove your credibility.

i-phone

The main aspect of Instagram marketing is to post pictures. Instead of going in for expensive cameras buy an iOS or Android phone. I-Phone is the best option as images captured and processed are clear and attractive. iOS cameras are superior in quality.

Watermark your pictures

Add watermark or imark on your pictures. This will help to keep photo theft away from your profile. Have your logo on each and every picture. Let it be mute in the background or visible in the middle.

Kik Messenger

Once your account becomes popular and you start to get heavy traffic spam is likely to occur. You'll be bombarded with unwanted spam. Kik messenger helps to weed it out.

hashtags

The posting quality of your pictures and content should be top class. Hashtag the keywords. Let them be descriptive. Have more than five hashtags for every picture.

Timing

Timing is very important. Post pictures either in the evenings or during lunch time. That is the time when people check their phones. Weekends are also an ideal time to advertise. Don't post 10 pictures in a day. Keep it at 2 or 3. Post two to three products of the same kind together. This will give people the choice to choose.

Be personal

Add content that makes it personal. People like to see such posts where they feel included.

Grow your impact

Unless you grow your impact on social media you'll not be able to sell. Be it Facebook or Twitter or Instagram growing your presence is very important. There are several tools available to do this. Instead of depending on others to help you gain visibility, do it yourself. Self-help is the best option. Here are some steps you need to take to grow your impact on social media.

- Interaction is the foremost aspect of promotion. Talk to your customers on

Facebook, Twitter, Instagram and other platforms. Like posts and pictures that are similar to your product and interact with people in the comments section. This will help you to participate in the communication.

- Have contests, events and give gifts. This will help to grow your customer base. It'll also show you as a genuine seller.
- Use hashtags to build contacts. Keywords and has tags have become popular tools to sell on social media.
- Keep an eye out for trends. Use latest techniques.
- Ask your audience for inputs. That'll help you to improve as well as communicate with them.
- Identify high influencers in your niche. Connect with them and ask them to review your product too. Their followers will be able to see your products and that'll help you to gain more visibility

Chapter 7 - Wrapping up social media with newsletters and PR

Email marketing is dead. Or is it? There are claims and counter claims. Meanwhile, email newsletters are becoming more sophisticated. Tools like Mailchimp can elevate your newsletter experience to a different level altogether. Combining newsletters with your social media campaign can be highly effective. Email marketing can tell you about your customers more than any other marketing tool. It engages the customer at a different personalized level. People still want to receive information tailor-made for them. They want to be pampered and feel wanted. This part of human nature will never change – people or customers will reciprocate enthusiastically if you offer them personalized service.

Success in social media marketing is a result of your ability to coordinate all online activities seamlessly. This will result in a different level of customer satisfaction. Look at the big picture and don't fall in love with a single platform in exclusion of others. Consider newsletters as an integral part of your social media campaign. Consistency in customer experience is critical. Your customer must feel at home whether they are interacting with you on Facebook or browsing through your e-commerce site. Give your customers a comfort zone and they will park themselves there. This is for sure.

There are many other advantages to a comprehensive marketing strategy. Your marketing team, whether it is working on your social media efforts or on your newsletters, will be more efficient. There will not be any duplication of work and effort. All of you will speak with the same voice and tone. Your customers will also get a seamless experience. It has been seen that team members feel more comfortable when working in a cohesive, holistic environment. The message you convey will be clear and lucid. Your branding effort will bear fruit quickly if you follow this strategy.

As such, you have to answer some vital questions before launching an integrated campaign. There are some features of email marketing which you may not find in social media platforms. Personalization is one such feature. Everyone is treated equally when you are on Facebook. There is no differentiation. The personal touch is missing. On the other hand, you can make your campaign go viral on Facebook which is impossible through email marketing. You have to understand the nuances of each platform and capitalize on their individual strength.

Combining social media and newsletter campaigns together usually leads to confusion unless you get everyone on the same page. Synchronizing activities is an important activity which can reduce cross-talk. The social media team may be using tools which are different from those used by the newsletter team. You may be sending off newsletters which are totally out of sync with your Facebook campaign. The customer is obviously confused when such things happen. Duplication of activities is another byproduct of asynchronous processes. Maybe there is a possibility of consolidation between various teams. Your email team can directly lift material from your Facebook content and vice versa.

Campaigns should be seamless and this can happen only if everyone in your team is talking the same language. There is no need to spend on a costly tool. You can use Google calendar, spreadsheets and files to create a seamless team. Another advantage of using Google Docs is that the files are updated online and your team members can work on the same document sitting in different places around the globe.

Creating a list

It's quite a task to create an email list. Getting followers on Facebook is an equally tough task. Why don't you exchange your lists between your email campaign and social media? Your social media marketing campaign should allow users to sign up to your email list. This is easier said than done. People dislike opting for lists unless they find a distinct advantage. It's a good policy to provide incentives, in the form of free downloads or discounts on product pricing, to entice prospective customers to sign up. Your Facebook faithful need something exciting to agree with you. You can run promotional campaigns through newsletters and promote them on Facebook and twitter.

It's also an excellent idea to upload your email list to social media platforms. Eventually, you have to optimize your customer lists. Cross-fertilization works well in the context of social media. A short burst of promotion through Twitter, followed by a medium-term Facebook campaign and backed by newsletters can take you far into social media territory.

Creating Social Media and PR campaigns

Public relations have undergone a metamorphosis online. It has become more potent and much more powerful than traditional

PR. The reason is clear- the reach has become tremendous and the PR net can be spread wide and far simply by clicking a button. If you call social media marketing as disruptive online PR is way above in potency. Combining social media and PR makes sense.

There can be no doubt that you can reach a huge audience by using Facebook, but the audience is diffused despite all your efforts to remain focused. With PR you can reach out to influencers – those who are trendsetters with a huge fan following. You should attend conferences and events which are specific to your trade. Building relations with trade partners gas many benefits. You have to be respected by your peers if you want to be acknowledged in your field.

You don't have to put extra effort to create content for your public relations effort. Pick up existing content and repurpose for your PR campaigns. You can also do the opposite – take your PR content and repurpose for your social media platforms. You can transform your PR content into infographics or even a video for your YouTube. Your PR material can be spun off to create content for social media channels, for newsletters, YouTube videos, Short and sweet tweets etc.

PR efforts lead to endorsements which are pretty valuable to build a reputation. Imagine that you as an apparel manufacturer are mentioned in a post by Gucci – your sales will hit the roof. PR is, therefore, a powerful tool in your social media marketing arsenal.

Chapter 8 - Mobile Marketing

Social media on mobile
Harvesting leads & sales from mobile
Wonders of WhatsApp

Social media on mobile

Phones were & still are used only to communicate till a decade ago. The arrival of mobiles marked the social media revolution and transformed the way businesses marketed their products. A single SMS was widely circulated and made millions of people aware of the latest developments and your business offers. In the year 2000, it was only mobile phones with SMS facility that was used by businesses. With the advent of smartphones, the market exploded and allowed everybody to advertise through mobile. I-Phone, Blackberry, Samsung and various other brands jumped on the bandwagon and offered internet on their phones.

The number of applications available on smartphones is mind boggling as you can not only communicate but market and sell your products directly to customers. Carpooling has also got an application wherein you give your details and someone close to your area picks you up and drops. Uber the taxi service app started this trend and today it is benefitting millions of people to get a ride. In case you wish to order food online there is an app that'll enable you to pay online and order food. The food reaches your doorstep before you reach home. Pet food, grocery, veggies can all be ordered through your smartphones. GPS enables you to track your loved ones to see if they've reached their destination safely. Tracking of vehicles has made several women feel safe around the world. This humble mobile phone acts like a wonder instrument in your hands. When people see any untoward incident in public all they do is take video and make it go viral on social media. Thieves, molesters, and criminals are caught thanks to smart mobiles.

An application called RedLaser on I-phones enables you to scan the barcode from supermarkets and compare the price with an online store. There are mobile apps that enable you to conduct banking online. Virtual banks like PayPal enable you to make purchases online and pay through your phone. Sitting in the cool comfort of your home or office you can conduct all transactions with your mobile. This simple device acts like a weapon in the hands of journalists. They're able to pass on news and information within no time all around the world. Realizing the power of mobile, social media giants like Facebook, Twitter and Instagram made themselves available on the mobile platform. A mobile became the battleground for marketing products.

There are more than 140,000 applications available on I-phone. Android phones have millions of applications. It is very easy to use these apps. Go to Google store on your phone and download. In future, your mobile may also act like a remote control switch for your garage and household appliances.

Laura's office on the go

Laura is a freelance web designer who is a member in several freelancing platforms across the web. All of them have mobile applications and Laura has downloaded the sites she works in onto her mobile. So wherever Laura goes her office goes with her. She gets mobile alerts on her phone when a client tries to contact her or send an invite to a job. Her phone beeps and alerts her. She responds to clients' right from where she's either traveling or eating lunch at a cafeteria. She even communicates while attending a wedding or watching a movie. She can even transfer money from her freelancer account to her bank. Literally, her virtual office is in her hands.

Smartphones have made people go dumb is a cynical way of looking at it. Since your phone alerts you when someone calls or texts or has sent a video you no longer waste time on remembering birthdays.

Harvesting leads & sales from mobile

Lead generation is a strategy that creates interest in a product with the goal to make a sale. With the advent of mobiles, lead generation has taken a different complexion altogether. Though every business owner is aware of the lead generation he doesn't know how to go about it. Mostly businesses bombard customers with emails, newsletters and lengthy phone calls which put him away. Where is the time for people to go through a lengthy email?

The online and mobile techniques are different from the conventional techniques. Mobiles and social media use different strategies to get leads. There are 4 'L's that are required for a successful online marketing strategy. They are Lead capture, Lead magnets, Landing page conversion and lead scoring. Though these leads can get the customer to the buy page to make him buy you need to have compelling content and a robust product. That depends totally on the quality of the product.

Though mobile marketing enables you to reach the customer ultimately he has to arrive at your website to make the purchase.

When people go on the landing page they look at the 'call to action' button. Focus only on that and cut the crap. Don't have too much information on the landing page, remember they are repeated customers and referrals that will jack up your sales.

Whether you're a small business or an individual your mobile can double up as an office too. If you're selling products or offering services you can buy mobile numbers from phone operators for a fee and send bulk SMS's. You can also control your social media accounts through mobile. Domino's the pizza chain uses mobile marketing to inform customers about their discounts and free schemes. They also offer a coupon code that can be redeemed while ordering pizza. Mobile numbers can be bought from malls, car parking lot, stores, and other outlets.

Mobile marketing has 100% reach, unlike email marketing. For example, if you send 10,000 emails chances are only 50% of them will open and read it. Whereas if you send 10,000 SMS's then you can be sure that all the recipients will read your messages. You can be assured that conversion rate in SMS marketing is much more than email marketing. Create trust with your customers by keeping their numbers with you and not further sell it. If you break the trust then unlikely they'll remain your customer. Instead, ask for permission upfront so that they're aware that you'll be sending offers and coupon codes.

Respect your customer's rights. If they don't wish to be disturbed with offers, stop sending them. Consumer rights in many countries advocate this.

The Wonders of WhatsApp

The year 2010 marked the advent of WhatsApp and everyone started using it on their smartphone. It was free and still is. Started by Brian Acton and Jan Koum, initially, it was used by people to talk and connect. WhatsApp transformed a couple of years ago when Facebook purchased it and offered video calling, group chat rooms, Image and video sharing, etc. today there are more than a billion users on WhatsApp from 180 different countries. Isn't it a mind-boggling figure?

WhatsApp is a great platform to advertise and make your product known to customers. It is very easy to start groups on WhatsApp. When you advertise on social media or a customer arrives at your website and fills in the sign-up form with a mobile number on your site you can connect with them through WhatsApp. The only warning is to totally avoid spamming customers; Chances of getting blocked by them is high. Ask first if they wish to see your catalog. Only on getting their consent will you then send across your products.

WhatsApp is a great way to connect. When you see items for sale on Facebook or Twitter, ask for the phone number and speak personally. This way you get a bargain if you need to. Also, you can send bank details through WhatsApp rather than putting it on Facebook, putting your personal info out there publicly is never recommended After making payment or receiving the courier you can still be in touch with the seller/ buyer. Only, make sure that the people involved are genuine and mean business. They shouldn't be the kind who will take the money and scoot. Make sure that they're genuine before dealing with businesses as well as customers on social media.

A new feature has been added to WhatsApp a few days ago. Like Snap Chat, you can make a story and post it so that all your contacts can see. Here, you can showcase your products one by one. Interested people can ask for the price and make payment so that you can send them the product. It is that simple!

There are software's available that can send bulk messages that are customized with the recipient's name, city, and phone number. You can also conduct polls through WhatsApp. You can be assured that the person has received it as you get to see if they've seen the message or not. It is indeed interesting to note that mobile marketing and WhatsApp have taken the world by storm and people are constantly on their phone 24/7. Whether you're a plumber, a small businessman or a corporate honcho, you cannot just do away with or avoid mobile marketing. They're here to stay, and in a couple of years, can even change the course of conventional marketing.

Chapter 9 - Social media metrics

Tom Barrow was a good hotelier – that's what he thought. He had worked his way up from a humble waiter to the exalted position of cashier. Tom had good taste and good friends. One day, he casually mentioned that he wanted to set up a restaurant and was surprised to know that his friends were ready to back him up. Why not? He was a hard working guy and knew the restaurant business. Tom chucked his job from the restaurant he had worked in for more than a decade. These were heavy days for him. Though he was confronted with many difficulties, his enthusiasm saw him sail through rough waters. Finally, the day came when he launched his upscale restaurant in downtown New York. 'The Hub' made a huge splash in the area and when customers poured into his restaurant, Tom was not surprised.

Tom felt that the business had taken off like a rocket. The cash register rang constantly while customers had to book a table in advance. Tom dreamt of starting another restaurant soon. His friends were ecstatic with the success of their venture. Life was good for Tom.

One month flew by in euphoric excitement and it was time to take stock. This is when Tom felt the first shock. 'The Hub' was running at a loss and a considerable one. How could this happen, Tom asked himself. The restaurant was always full and the customers were delighted with the food and service. In fact, he had received some glorious feedback from customers. Looking back, Tom could not think of a single wrong step in the past month. Digging deep into his accounts, he soon realized that the overheads and the exorbitant rent were the main reason for the debacle. Could Tom have avoided the losses? Was there a possibility to get back into the black after entering the sea of red?

Can you see the similarity between 'The Hub' and your social media venture? You must know what is happening inside your campaign than purely relying on some easily available data. As a social media marketer, you have immediate access to data. In fact, you are swimming in data. Yet, you may be misled like Tom when it comes to the health of your online business. In internet parlance, visitor count is only a small sign of your overall campaign success. Tom was not wrong to assume that footfalls determine the level of activity. Still, his business experienced a net loss. The amount of data you are dealing with on social media is humungous. You are engaging with your audience on a day to day, hour to hour basis. You are faced with a problem of plenty. You don't know how to use the data productively. What data to use and how much to discard is the art of metrics. There are several indicators which you must follow regularly to assess your health. What matters most to your business is what you must monitor. The rest you must discard.

What do you mean by reach?

Unlike a brick and mortar establishment, there is no limit to the traffic which you can accommodate. In fact, for online ventures, the more the merrier. For Tom, the limitation was in the form of space. Was it possible for him to increase his customers? What he noticed was that some prospective customers went back because they could not find a place to sit in his restaurant. Maybe he could have looked at takeaways? For an online venture, reach is an important metric. The growth rate is an indicator of how well you are resonating with your audience. You have to maintain a healthy growth rate because social media is volatile. Many customers will find other interesting places to visit and this vacuum must be filled by new customers.

Tom could have evaluated the number of customers who did not engage with him and instead opted to walk out rather than waiting for a table. Tom could have learned from the growth or fall in engagement, had he used the metrics more prudently. For a website, traffic alone is not a good indicator of success. Engagement has a finality to it. It shows how well you are interacting with customers and how they are responding to it.

Another metric which sheds light on your social media marketing effectiveness is return rate and frequency. How many times your followers revisit your site is an excellent indicator of your progress. Getting people to return requires constant effort. Your efforts MUST be to keep your content fresh and lively if you wish the same set of people to visit again and again. You must be able to differentiate between repeat and new visitors. Your ability to engage the audience will be reflected by the number of repeat visitors.

In the end, what matters is the sale. Did your visitor buy your product or simply walked through? This metric is the most important because the buck stops here. This is also called conversion rate. There are many reasons why you may find a healthy rise in visitor count and great engagement numbers, but very few converts into actual customers. One of the reasons is the security issue. People don't have faith in payment gateways and are scared that their bank details may be compromised. In some instances, buyers cannot locate the 'BUY' button. This may seem improbable but nonetheless, it's a reality. This is a failure of the user interface. Conversion is a delicate matter also because your visitors are wooed by your competitors. They may go for a discount offered by your competitor at that point in time.

You must have specific conversion goals and measure them through various tools like Google Analytics. Conversion rates reveal the true picture about your marketing effort. It is the culmination of your strategy.

Now that we have scanned through some important metrics, let's look at some specific social media analytics.

Facebook Analytics

Did you know that Facebook has a comprehensive analytics tool which tells you almost everything you need to know about how your Facebook pages are performing? A Facebook insight is also intuitive and easy to use. You have to get used to the terminology and the rest is as easy as having a cake ..well almost.

You can begin with the Page you want to get insights on. In addition to the overview, you can drill down to the specifics if you are interested. There are many instances when business owners have simply got lost inside the metrics and have never emerged from it. Humor apart, you must make sure that this is in the end metrics. You need a human brain to analyze and understand the numbers. Don't spend too much time delving into the statistics.

The best place on Facebook insights is the overview tab. It provides you with the most important metrics. You can view the number of page likes, which will give you a broad picture of your social engagement. Needless to say, that page likes are the most important metrics. You can even compare your performance in the past seven days with that of the previous week. This number is important because you must keep showing improvement in page views. Post Reach is a metric which tells you the total number of people who have viewed your content in any form – Pages or Ads.

There are a number of ways in which your audience interacts with your Facebook page. These may include clicks, likes, comments or shares during the previous week. This is called engagement. You may be able to infer different things and reach different conclusions from these individual metrics.

Many businesses are happy with the data gleaned from the overview tab, which is not correct. A very important part of Facebook metrics is information on your posts. You can get complete data regarding your five previous posts.

Reach and engagement tells you about how your post is faring in the sea of plenty. Obviously, your posts will only be read if you make them interesting enough. You can applaud your efforts if you have a healthy metrics. Alternately you would know what went wrong with your effort and try to make amends in later posts. You can drill down further and reach the juiciest part – your competitor's pages. You can closely watch your competitor in action and cry or laugh as appropriate. You can see total page likes, new posts, and engagement. This is a good place to spend some time, assuming that your competitors know more than you about social media marketing.

Twitter Analytics

Twitter is an integral part of social media marketing and twitter analytics is an unavoidable tool to understand your performance. You don't have to worry much because you have the convenience of Twitter analytics dashboard.

Twitter analytics dashboard provides you with some vital information which tells you whether you have done well or failed miserably in your Twitter campaign. Of course, the number of tweets conveys nothing since you already have this information. Impressions give you an idea how popular your tweet had been by indicating the number of people who have seen it. Profile visits indicate your popularity. At least someone wants to know who you are! Mentions goes a little further – shows how many times you have been mentioned by others in their tweets. You can expect this number to grow if you are a movie star about to win the Oscars. Otherwise, mentions are a cause for celebration. Followers are the good Samaritans who want to know your thoughts. Retweets are another reason for you to smile. Retweets are what you are actually hunting for when you want to sell something useful. Replies are events to be thankful for.

Overall, Twitter analytics is certainly worth a look.

Google Analytics

Google analytics is the biggest and best analytics tool ever created in this universe. It can tell you everything you need to know and more. You must know Google analytics if you want to succeed in social media marketing.

Though Google analytics covers all subjects under the earth, you will be more interested in Social Referrals. This place will show you how good or bad your social media marketing performance has been. You will get metrics like the sessions, page views, Average session duration, pages viewed per session etc. If you look at the social conversion report, you will learn about how people arrived at your site.

The first thing on your agenda before creating your social media marketing strategy should be to learn Google analytics. Otherwise, you will be like one of the five blind men trying to imagine an elephant by touching its different parts.

Conclusion

Now that you've read this book, you can confidently go all out and start your social media campaign to promote products online. Businesses need to understand and accept that there is a community there out on social media and that is here to stay. Harnessing the power of it lies totally with the businesses. It is up to you to decide how you'll extract information about users and communicate with them without being overly imposing on them. After all, you can get blocked or spammed easily. Maintaining your reputation as well as reaching out to customers is an art unto itself. By marrying your social media presence with your customers, you're guaranteed ongoing success as a business.

From traditional marketing, moving online will help to keep you up with the times. Platforms like Facebook, twitter, Instagram, LinkedIn, Tumblr are all amazing sites where you have a ready-made market for your products. YouTube is another powerful medium that has created many celebrities and millionaires. That is the power of social media. People don't join social media to buy stuff or associate with a brand. They join to share their pictures, stories and connect with people. They like to socialize and be seen and heard. Make it your top priority for your product to smoothly blend with this idea. This is when it will be noticeable. Choose your products wisely and promote them on social media. Make sure that your product is wholesome and caters to a wide audience. Engage people and offer incentives to join your community. That is when you'll be seen, heard and appreciated.

Thank you for reading this book!

www.ingramcontent.com/pod-product-compliance
Lightning Source LLC
Chambersburg PA
CBHW071444180526
45170CB00001B/450